UNWRAPPED

GINA GUDDAT
and the
F.I.T. Decisions
Team of Experts

UNWRAPPED

Real Questions
Asked by Real Girls

(about sex)

Providence House Publishers
PROVIDENCE PUBLISHING CORPORATION
FRANKLIN, TENNESSEE

Printed in the United States of America

11   10   09   08   07   1   2   3   4   5

Library of Congress Control Number: 2006939776

ISBN: 978-1-57736-388-0

Cover concept and photograph by Angela Mathena
Cover and page design by LeAnna Massingille

PROVIDENCE HOUSE PUBLISHERS
an imprint of
Providence Publishing Corporation
238 Seaboard Lane • Franklin, Tennessee 37067
www.providence-publishing.com
800-321-5692

conTenTs

contents

preface

Over the last several years, F.I.T. Decisions has been collecting questions from girls like you. From Seattle to New York, from Omaha to Orlando, teens have lots of questions about sex. The problem is, nobody really knows who to ask. If you can talk to your mom about this type of personal thing . . . great! It would be awesome if we could all learn about sex from our parents. It would be even greater if our parents knew all the answers to our questions. But nobody knows everything, so we thought, *Why not ask the experts?*

We compiled hundreds of questions and handed them over to the "sex experts." Well, actually, they are nurses and educators that specialize in this kind of stuff. These women have the training and the medical experience needed to answer the toughest questions.

Some of the same questions were asked over and over again, which tells us that girls everywhere need answers. Unfortunately, movies, TV shows, and magazines are giving us the wrong information. We hope this book will take away a lot of the guessing and confusion surrounding sex. Our goal is to teach the truth, and to reinforce the fact that sex truly is a marvelous gift from God when used in the context it was designed for.

WhY DOn'T GUYS TALK to YOU AbOUT HOW THEY FEEL?

Answer:
Because their brains are different than ours.

Let's Talk

The human brain is divided into two halves, the left hemisphere and the right hemisphere. The two sides are connected by a bridge called the corpus callosum. The right side specializes in spatial stuff like building things, judging distances (like how far a baseball will go when you throw it), and calculating things. The left side specializes in verbal stuff like talking, reading, and writing. Guys have stronger right brains and girls have stronger left brains. This means that although guys are usually better at constructing a tree house or fixing a car, girls are much better at analyzing their feelings and describing their emotions.

Girls can do it ALL!

When a baby is born, its brain is definitely either male or female. Not only is one hemisphere of the brain more active than the other, the bridge between the two halves also works differently. A female's corpus callosum is much larger. This means that she can move back and forth between the two sides of her brain amazingly fast. She can even use both sides of her brain at the same time. Basically, girls are able to multi-task. They can watch TV, talk on the phone, eat, and write an essay all at the same time.

Guys are just biologically different. The bridge between the two hemispheres of a guy's brain is much smaller. He tends to stay on the right side and doesn't switch back and forth as easily. This makes him more likely to focus on only one *task* at a time. Don't even try to talk to a guy while he is watching TV—it's impossible. Wait until the commercial.

Guys Do Have Feelings

Usually guys are not very verbal. If a guy isn't talking to you, it doesn't mean he's mad at you. Guys do have feelings and emotions; they just tend to keep them to themselves. Most guys cannot deal with their emotions along with something else at the same time. Because they are singularly focused, they may store the feeling away until later when they have time to

> Each day a guy speaks between two thousand to four thousand words, while a girl speaks six thousand to eight thousand words.

deal with it. For them, emotions are problems that need to be solved. Sometimes guys don't want (or know how) to talk to you about how they feel . . . but you should still ask.

Men are from Mars, Women are from Venus.

—John Gray, Author

Does MAKiNG OUT couNT as SEX?

Answer:
No. Making out, by definition, is prolonged kissing and touching. So making out doesn't count as sex.

Let's Talk

Even though making out doesn't count as sex, to a guy, making out is the road that leads to sex. Making out may make you feel cuddly and intimate, but for a guy, making out just makes him want sex. This desire for more, more, and more is called lust. A guy full of lust can make a lot of stupid decisions. When all he's thinking about is

getting more, he's *not* thinking about whether or not he loves you. He is not thinking about what will happen if you get pregnant, whether he wants you to be his only girlfriend, or whether he wants to marry you some day. He's certainly not thinking about supporting you or a child—he's only thinking about satisfying his desire for sex.

Draw Your Boundary Line

Prolonged kissing and touching is crossing the boundary line into unsafe territory. Why? The steps toward intimacy are progressive. One step leads to another. Making out is foreplay, which leads to sex, which was originally designed for marriage. When you start down the path of intimacy, you should be able to enjoy all that God has planned for you—within a marriage relationship. It's not wise to tempt yourself or your boyfriend by making out. Draw your physical boundary line and stick to it.

Passion is the quickest to develop,
and the quickest to fade.
Intimacy develops more slowly, and
commitment more gradually still.

—Robert Sternberg,
Psychology Professor, Yale University

DON'T TOUCH!

WHy does it MaTTer WhaT YOU WEAR?

Answer:
Although what's inside is more important than what's outside, the reality is, people usually treat you according to the way you dress.

Let's Talk

Guys are no different. They are visual creatures, so they respond to the way you're dressed. What seems to you like a fashionably low-cut shirt seems to a guy like an invitation to handle the merchandise. Sorry girls, but God created guys to be visual. They like what they see, which is great when it's your husband who's looking only at you. But guys are stimulated by just about anything with a pulse! This doesn't mean your sense of fashion has to be thrown out the window. It *does* mean you need to use your brain and choose your clothes carefully. You can still look fantastic and stylish without showing your boobs, buns, or belly.

Power Dressing

Take responsibility and recognize that your clothing choices are powerful! Choose to wear clothes that focus his attention on your face, not your private parts. If he's focusing on your face, he'll get to know you and treat you like a person instead of an object. Guys are confused by tight or sexy clothes. Show a little skin, their hormones take over, and all logic is out the window.

Know your body type, and dress in what makes you look and feel best. In the dressing room, test new outfits from every angle. Lean over and make sure nobody can see down your shirt or up your skirt. Be discreet and choose your clothes carefully, because they influence how others perceive you. If you feel good about yourself, you don't have to try to get attention by showing off your bod.

Logic

What a man enjoys about a woman's clothes
are his fantasies of how
she would look without them.

—Brendan Francis, Irish Playwright

HO**W** d**o** **y**o**u** S**T**a**y** PURe **?**

Answer:

Guard your heart, your mind, and your actions. Staying pure is a choice. It is a daily process that starts today and affects the rest of your life. Purity involves every part of you: your heart, mind, body, and spirit.

Let's Talk

The bottom line is that whatever you choose to put into your heart and mind will come out in your actions. It's the old motto: "You reap what you sow."

That means that whatever seed you put into the garden will determine what kind of plant is going to sprout up. If you plant pumpkins, you aren't going to get strawberries. It's the same with our lives. First, you sow a thought, then you reap a deed; sow a deed, reap a habit; sow a habit, reap a character; sow a character, reap a destiny. This is how it plays out:

Sow a Thought: You watch a movie that shows people having sex.

Reap a Deed: Next time you're with your boyfriend, you are tempted to have sex.

Sow a Deed: You have sex.

Reap a Habit: It's easier to have sex with the next guy.

Sow a Habit: You now have sex regularly.

Reap a Character: People start to call you a slut.

Sow a Character: You now have a bad reputation.

Reap a Destiny: You get pregnant, your boyfriend leaves you, and you're a single mom.

YIKES!

Do not be deceived: God cannot be mocked. A man reaps what he sows. The one who sows to please his sinful nature, from that nature will reap destruction.

—New Testament Bible, Galatians 6:7–8

Don't Set Yourself Up

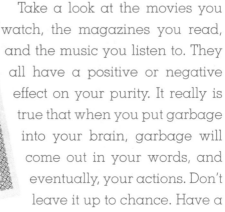

Take a look at the movies you watch, the magazines you read, and the music you listen to. They all have a positive or negative effect on your purity. It really is true that when you put garbage into your brain, garbage will come out in your words, and eventually, your actions. Don't leave it up to chance. Have a strategy that will help you stay pure.

Your eyes

Stay away from Internet pornography. Don't watch R-rated movies with sex scenes and avoid trashy magazines.

Your ears

Listen to music that lifts your spirit. Stay away from music with sexual, depressing, or degrading lyrics.

Your body

Be careful what you wear. No showing boobs, buns, crotches, or anything else that turns on a guy. Keep your private parts private! Know where you stand on purity and live like it!

Finally, [sisters], whatever is true,
whatever is noble, whatever is right,
whatever is pure, whatever is lovely,
whatever is admirable—if anything is excellent
or praiseworthy—think about such things.
—New Testament Bible, Philippians 4:8

Why is Pre MARITAL Sex bad, and Why does the CHURCH SAY IT'S SiNFUl?

Answer:

Premarital sex has a lot of risks. Sex, the most intimate human act, is intended to be enjoyed within the safety of marriage. Having premarital sex is like taking something before it rightfully belongs to you.

Let's Talk

Sex is good. It bonds two people together to become one. It's awesome! Having sex before you are married is the part that is not so good. Sex is designed to be enjoyed freely in a relationship that is permanent. Premarital sex robs you of the highest form of physical expression you can give your husband. It robs you of the incredible bond of being one with only your husband. You will be physically bonded to any guys you are sexually intimate with.

Premarital sex has emotional consequences, too. It can change the focus of a relationship in a big way. What if your boyfriend tells all of his friends about it? People might start talking about you behind your back. Then there is the nagging fear of getting caught in the act.

Basically, having sex can make you an emotional wreck, and who wants that? Once you are married, you will have freedom from guilt, shame, and regret. Additionally, you'll have the freedom of not comparing or being compared to anyone else.

Sex Is Powerful

The Christian Bible, Jewish Torah, and Islamic Qur'an all teach that premarital sex is wrong.

That is why some people call it sin. Sex is powerful! If used incorrectly, it has the power to destroy life. When used correctly, it has the ability to give life. Sex is meant to be a good thing, honorable and pure.

Sex is a shortcut to everything.

—Anne Cumming, *The Love Quest*

What are the MOST Common STDs?

Answer:

The most serious STDs (sexually transmitted diseases) are:

> **Chlamydia**
> **Gonorrhea**
> **Hepatitis B**
> **Herpes Simplex II**
> **HIV/AIDS**
> **Human Papilloma Virus (HPV)**
> **Syphilis**
> **Trichomoniasis**

Let's Talk

Any STD you can get in the genital area you can also get in the mouth, throat, and lungs. HIV/AIDS, HPV, hepatitis, and herpes are viruses. There is no cure for a virus. You can treat the symptoms, but you can never kill the virus. HIV/AIDS, HPV, hepatitis B, chlamydia, gonorrhea, and syphilis often infect and damage parts of your internal organs before

FACT: In a single act of unprotected sex, a teenage girl has a 1 percent risk of getting HIV, a 50 percent risk of acquiring gonorrhea, and a 30 percent risk of contracting genital herpes.

they even show any outward symptoms of infection. Plus, you can't always see an STD on a person's body. Once you have an STD, it's easy to pass it on. If you have sex with a guy, <u>you are being exposed to all the diseases of everyone he has ever been with.</u>

> To be intimate with a foolish [man] is like going to bed with a razor.
>
> —Benjamin Franklin, *Poor Richard's Almanac*

Why has SEX become the THING to Do?

Answer:

Sex is everywhere in the media. People use it to numb the pain in their lives and don't even realize the consequences it can bring.

Let's Talk

Sex is everywhere. It's portrayed as the ultimate experience we can all have anytime we want! Advertisers use it to sell their products. We hear about sex in the songs we listen to, TV shows we see, and movies we watch. Sex is on billboards and road signs, and we read about it in magazines and books. The word "sexy" is used to describe almost everything in our society, from cars to toothpaste. Sexy phrases are printed across the front of T-shirts and the backside of sweatpants and shorts. The main reason why sex has become the thing to do is that it is constantly in our faces! It does seem like everyone is doing it.

Nobody Talks About the Consequences

People are being taught that there are no consequences to sex. Everything we read, hear, and see from the media says that sex outside of marriage is normal, acceptable, and even expected. Women's bodies are portrayed as nothing more than sexual playthings to be used for casual recreation. Today's culture tells us, "If sex feels good to you, do it. If it works for you, do it. If it gives you the advantage, go for it." The moral standard of what is sexually right and wrong has changed.

FACT

Not everybody is doing it!
Only one-quarter of ninth graders are having sex, and only one-half of seventeen-year-olds are. That means that most teens are not havng sex.

Like a Drug

People use sex to numb the hurt and pain in their lives. Sex is like a drug; it can make you forget your problems for a while. Sex can easily become a way to feel good instantly. Unfortunately, it's only temporary. Using sex to ease your hurt is like using a Band-Aid to cover up a deep wound. Rather than getting surgery to fix the issue, you take the easy way out and prevent yourself from really healing. If you've got emotional baggage, seek help! If you're just trying to fit in, take a stand! Choose to rise above the crowd. Instead of letting sex become the thing to do in your life, choose to do things differently. And remember, the majority of girls aren't having sex.

> Ninety-three percent of sexually active teens say they first had sex voluntarily. At least one-quarter to one-half of them also say they regret it!

FACT

Love in young men is not for the most part love, but lust, [and its accomplishment is the end].

—Miguel de Cervantes, *Don Quixote* (paraphrase)

IF YOU'RE IN LOVE, IS IT OK TO HAVE PREMARITAL SEX?

Answer:
No.

Let's Talk

Love is a decision. You choose to love every day of your life. Love is a word that expresses commitment and action based on giving. You may feel like you are in love, and therefore want to give yourself permission to have sex. But premarital sex is really based on taking. If you are not married, the guy you are having sex with is taking something from you that doesn't belong to him. Premarital sex is not right because there's no commitment, and it's not based on a permanent, true commitment. It's most likely based on a simple physical attraction (otherwise known as lust!).

Chemistry

Ever wonder why people move in and out of relationships so quickly? Everyone loves feeling "in love." These feelings come from a chemical in the brain called dopamine. We should not confuse this stage of a relationship with real love, which comes with a commitment.

All of those crazy feelings and emotions you experience when you are infatuated with a hot guy really come from dopamine. When you are in the midst of a dopamine rush, you feel great. You have lots of energy and usually need very little food and very little sleep. Unfortunately, this brain chemical usually runs out after one-and-a-half to three-and-a-half years—sometimes sooner!

Don't be deceived. Don't allow your boyfriend to take something away from you in the name of love. When he says, "If you love me, you'll have sex with me," recognize that this is not love. He's trying to *get*, not give. When he says, "Just let me do it this one time," don't fall for it.

He is trying to get what he wants in order to satisfy his own physical desires. He is not thinking about giving to you. This is not love. Most guys actually break up with girls after they have sex with them. They move on to their next conquest.

Eight Ways to Tell If You're In Love

1. *True love distinguishes between a person and a body.*
2. *True love is always respectful.*
3. *True love is self-giving.*
4. *True love can grow without physical expression.*
5. *True love seeks to build a relationship.*
6. *True love embraces responsibility.*
7. *True love can postpone gratification.*
8. *True love is basically commitment.*

—Erwin W. Lutzer, Moody Church
Senior Pastor, Teacher, Author, and Radio Personality

Guys Versus Girls

Guys and girls experience relationships differently. Guys give love to get sex. Girls give sex to get love. When a guy says he loves a girl and wants to have sex, the girl gets hung up on the emotions. She's thinking about romance, a future wedding, decorating her first home, and what she will name her kids someday. All the guy is thinking about is when he's going to get "it" again. He's not thinking about commitment, responsibility, or marriage.

Choose to take control of your emotions. If you don't manage them, they will manage you. Love is a commitment, not a feeling. Choose to save yourself, and then marry and commit to someone who really loves you.

Love is patient and kind.
Love is not jealous or boastful or proud or rude.
Love does not demand its own way.
Love is not irritable, and it keeps no record of when it has been wronged.
It is never glad about injustice but rejoices whenever the truth wins out.
Love never gives up, never loses faith, is always hopeful, and endures through every circumstance. Love will last forever . . .

—New Testament Bible, 1 Corinthians 13:4–8a (NLT)

SHOULD a girl **MasturBate** SO SHE WON'T **BE TEMPtED** **2** HaVE **SeX** Before SHE gets MARRIEd?

Answer:
No. That's not really a solution.

Let's Talk

Although masturbation may relieve physical desires, it will not ultimately satisfy you. It will not meet your deep physical, emotional, and spiritual longings for intimacy. It's basically like having sex with yourself.

It's a Brain Thing

Masturbation is a brain thing. The chemicals released in the brain during sex are very powerful. So powerful that the repeated use of self-stimulation may damage your ability to respond normally to your husband someday. Your body may continue to require the same activities to become aroused even though you are married. The bad news is that masturbation can become like an addiction, and addictions are very difficult to break. In fact, contrary to popular belief, the desire to masturbate does not go away once you are married, especially if it has become a habit.

We accuse guys of looking at women lustfully and having fantasies, but girls can also struggle in the same way. Respect your boyfriend. Don't let your mind go there. Learn to identify your feelings and respond to them in a healthy way. Recognize your desire to be loved and valued. Don't ignore your feelings by doing something quick just to make them go away faster. Instead, stop and figure out the real reason you want to masturbate. Deal with your emotions in a positive way.

Learning to exercise self-control is part of growing and maturing. Self-control is involved in all aspects of life. Release your energy in a positive way. Endorphins, the body's natural "feel good" chemicals, are also produced when you exercise. When you are tempted, go for a bike ride, swim, or run. Play tennis with a friend or take your dog for a walk. All of these activities will help relieve stress and curb sexual desires.

Just as Death and Destruction are never
satisfied, so human desire is never satisfied.

—Jewish Torah and
Old Testament Bible, Proverbs 27:20 (NLT)

CaN you geT STDs the 1st time You HAVe Sex?

Answer:

Yes. If the person you have sex with has an STD or is a carrier, you can get an STD from him.

Let's Talk

Whether it's your first time or not, it only takes one time to get an STD. A virus or bacteria from one body infects another body. Actually, you don't even have to have sex to become infected. Any exchange of bodily fluids, as in oral sex or skin-to-skin contact, can transmit an STD from one person to another.

FACT

More than a hundred thousand women every year find out they can't have a baby because an STD has made them infertile.

> Every year in the United States, twelve million people are infected with an STD; three million are teens!

FACT

It Only Takes Once

When a girl chooses to have sex with a guy, she not only gets what he gives her, she also gets what other people might have given him. In other words, <u>when you choose to have sex with someone, it is like having sex with everyone else he's already had sex with.</u> Who knows where all those people have been? It would be nice to think that just one time wouldn't hurt. Unfortunately, it only takes one time, or even just a little skin-to-skin, to get an STD. Are you willing to take the risk?

> *Emotions are made to enjoy, but out of control they tend to destroy.*
>
> —Lyle Flinner

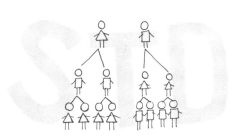

WHaT Do YoU do IF you FeEL like your FrieND, who is also a GiRL, is ComiNG oN 2 YOU?

Answer:

Go with your gut. If you feel uncomfortable by what she says or does, pay attention. You should probably cool the friendship. Confront your friend and tell her you don't like the level of intimacy. Honesty can bring true intentions to the surface. Let her know you are not interested in a lesbian relationship.

Let's Talk

Women enjoy close friendships, and they aren't afraid to show it. They express themselves by laughing and crying, hugging and giggling, working and hanging out together. There's nothing wrong with this. But if you start to feel weird around a close friend, you need to do something about it.

Strategies

Don't be alone with this girl. You can still be friendly to her, but avoid spending the night with her or getting too close. Stay away from rubbing each other's backs, or trying on clothes in front of each other. Avoid doing anything that might be interpreted as flirting. Experimenting or going down paths that lead to anything sexual in thought or action with either gender can lead to things you will regret. Your friend may be struggling with her own identity. If you think you can save your drowning friend, think again. She will just pull you under with her. Although you care about this girl, you can't be her life preserver. The best thing you can do for her is encourage her to get help.

Sexually confused, they abused and defiled
one another, women with women,
men with men—all lust, no love.

—*The Message Remix*, Romans 1:26

● ● ●● ● ●● ● ● ● ● ●● ● ● ● ● ● ●● ● ● ● ● ●● ● ● ●

If so **MaNY** people see **SEX** as
HORRiBLe,
WhY did **G**od create it **?**

Answer:

**God doesn't see sex as horrible. It
was His idea in the first place. He
designed sex for our pleasure and as
a way to reproduce so the human
race won't become extinct.**

Let's Talk

The Bible, the Torah, and the Qur'an say that
God is awesome. Therefore, everything God
created is good. God thought up sex. He designed
it to be the highest form of physical expression
between a husband and wife. The gift of sex is

so powerful that it has the ability to create life. Because it is so powerful, God gives us important guidelines. Sex is intended for a committed marriage relationship. When we don't follow God's guidelines concerning sex, there are serious consequences. What He designed to be good suddenly feels dirty and horrible.

> It is with our passions, as it is with
> fire and water, they are good servants
> but bad masters.
>
> —Aesop, Storyteller

We Are All Sexual Beings

While the media constantly encourages and promotes sex, it sometimes feels like churches, teachers, and parents are constantly trying to make teens afraid of sex. Adults mean well; they are just trying to prevent you from making a mistake that you will regret. But hey, let's face it—we are all sexual beings. Sex is critical for the continuation of the species. Sex is good! That is not the issue. It's all about the timing and the context in which you have sex. Remember, before you are married, it's all about how much of yourself you can save for your future husband. But inside marriage, it's an awesome benefit to enjoy!

> ### Don't excite love, don't stir it up, until the time is ripe—and you're ready.
>
> —Jewish Torah and *The Message Remix*,
> Song of Songs 2:7

How FaR is TOo FAr?

Answer:
Each person has to create her own boundaries.

Let's Talk

This may sound radical, but anything more than a simple kiss can easily go too far. The farther you go, the fuzzier the boundary lines become. Lots of women admit, "I wish I hadn't gone that far with guys before I got married. I feel like I was used." Nobody ever seems to say, "I just wish I had gone further." Decide right now what you will and won't do with a guy. Make a list. Here are some ideas:

Will Do

- Hang out together
- Hug
- Hold hands
- Simple kiss

Won't Do

- Sit on his lap
- See each other without clothes on
- Tongue
- Lay down next to each other
- Be alone with him
- Lick
- Make out
- Suck
- Rub up against each other
- Have oral sex
- Touch or be touched in those private places

Stay True to Your List

Trust yourself and stick to what you will and won't do. If a guy keeps pressuring you to do something that is on your "won't do" list, it's a no brainer . . . <u>he wants sex, not you!</u> A guy who respects your "no" is the guy who wants to get to know you as a person, not just a piece of flesh.

Do you not know that your body is a temple of the Holy Spirit, who is in you, whom you have received from God? You are not your own; you were bought at a price. Therefore honor God with your body.

—New Testament Bible, 1 Corinthians 6:19–20

What do you DO if you've already goNe TOO FaR?

Answer:

Forgive yourself and accept God's forgiveness. Forgive the guy you went too far with (whether it was your idea or his). Choose to start over right now!

Let's Talk

In order to get a different result, you have to be willing to do something new. If you want to be sexually pure, you have to go about things differently. You used to date certain guys, you used to go to certain parties, and you used do certain things with your body. Be willing to change some of the things you used to do. Get rid of the boyfriend you went too far with. Get rid of the crowd that gets you into trouble. If you don't want to go too far, don't hang around people who do.

If you have made mistakes, even serious ones,
there is always another chance for you.
What we call failure is not the falling down,
but the staying down.

—Mary Pickford, Actress

Pray you now, forget and forgive.

—William Shakespeare,
King Lear, act 4, scene 7

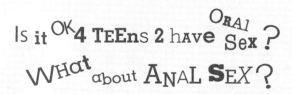

Is it OK 4 TEEns 2 have ORAl Sex?
WHat about ANAL SEX?

Answer:
No and no.

Let's Talk

Oral sex is **not** a safe way to have sex. It does not preserve your virginity and it does not come without consequences. Some girls believe if they can't get pregnant, it's not sex. But the medical definition of sex is any genital contact at all—whether hand to genitals, mouth to genitals, or genitals to genitals.

What Is Oral Sex Exactly?

Oral sex is the act of putting one's mouth, lips, or tongue on another person's genitals with the intention of sexually arousing and stimulating the other person to orgasm. Cunnilingus is the term for orally stimulating a woman's vulva and clitoris. Fellatio is the act of orally stimulating a man's penis.

A girl may begin having oral sex because she thinks everyone else is doing it, or because she is invited to a "party" where oral sex is performed in groups. She probably thinks it is innocent and there will be no emotional attachment. Unfortunately, afterwards a girl often feels shame, guilt, embarrassment, and regret.

FACT

If you have had oral sex, you are technically not a virgin.

Oral sex is intimate. It involves exposing a very special part of yourself to another person. It is an emotional experience and it can leave you feeling used and abused. There are emotional and social ramifications. Losing your reputation and your purity can happen quickly. Many girls suffer from poor self-esteem and even depression after engaging in oral sex.

Yuck—Warts in Your Mouth!

Any STD you can get in your genitals you can also get in your mouth. Anyone can get multiple STDs in her mouth and throat from having oral sex. Diseases such as chlamydia, syphilis, gonorrhea, HIV, herpes,

GROSS!

Anal sex also has its consequences. The anus was not made for penetration. Small tears in the blood vessels increase the risk of getting an infection. Hepatitis A and hepatitis B can be transmitted this way, as can HIV and AIDS. Half of all HIV diagnosed among boys age thirteen to nineteen were attributed to anal sex. Anal sex is not safe!

and HPV (human papilloma virus) grow and live in warm, moist, dark environments. Remember, a virus cannot be cured. Herpes and HPV are viruses that a girl will have to deal with in her mouth and throat for the rest of her life.

The body is a sacred garment.

—Martha Graham, Dancer

What is Chlamydia, and why is it SO DANGEROUS?

Answer:

Chlamydia is the most common bacterial STD in the United States, and affects teenage girls more than any other group in society. Although it is a bacterium, it has the characteristics of a virus. It can go undetected for a long time and damage your reproductive system before you even know it's there.

Let's Talk

Chlamydia is the silent killer of hopes and dreams! This STD affects millions of women each year. Some of these women go through a heartbreaking discovery when they get married and want to have a baby. They learn they can't have children, and go through extensive testing and even surgery to find out why they can't conceive. Then their doctors discover that their fallopian tubes are blocked because of chlamydia, which they never knew they even had! Unfortunately, there's nothing the doctors can do to reverse the damage caused by chlamydia.

Physical Symptoms

Some of the symptoms of chlamydia are abnormal discharge from the vagina, bleeding between periods, painful urination, severe abdominal pain, and high fever. Chlamydia has awful physical consequences. It can lead to pelvic inflammatory disease, tubal pregnancies, and as we said, it can even take away your ability to have kids! On the inside of your body, it looks like someone has poured glue into your fallopian tubes and uterus, causing them to become clogged. This means that the sperm can't travel through the tubes to fertilize the egg very well. Women who have had chlamydia may be sterile for life.

Safeguard the health both of body and soul.

—Cleobulus, Greek Sage

If a **Guy** **pressures** a girl to Have **S**$_{EX}$, what are **some** **ways** to get **OUT** of it ?

Answer:

Say _no_, then _go_! Get away from him and the situation. Don't waste time talking or explaining your views on sex—just go home or call your parents or friends to come get you. Avoid date rape!

Let's Talk

When a guy pressures you, he does not respect you. A guy who really cares about you will not make you feel like you have to do anything to earn his affection or love. Any guy you go out with should know where you stand on sex before marriage, and where you have drawn your boundary line. Even if it seems weird, explain your "won't do" list to him. Some girls wear purity jewelry as an outward symbol of their commitment. It's a great visual aid to open up the topic for discussion. Don't compromise your values or your boundaries for anyone.

Be Assertive

Plan to be in control. Carry your cell phone with you at all times. You might even consider taking a self-defense class. Practice being assertive by learning to say what you mean and mean what you say. If a guy pressures you, start your sentence with the word "No." Here's how to handle some of the most common pressure lines:

He says:

If you love me, you will have sex with me.

You say:

No, if you love me, you won't ask me to compromise.

He says:

Let's take our love to a higher level.

You say:

No, go take a hike.

Hi YAH!

He says:

Why not? You know you want me, baby.

You say:

No, what is it about the word "no" that you don't understand?

He says:

If you're not going to do this now, how do I know what you'll be like when we get married?

You say:

No, if you don't respect what I say now, I won't even be around when you finally want to get married.

He says:

Let's go to my house. No one else is home.

You say:

No, I don't want to. Let's go hang out with our friends.

Blessed is the [girl] that endureth temptation: for when [she] is tried, [she] shall receive the crown of life.

— New Testament Bible, James 1:12 (KJV)

No test or temptation that comes your way is beyond the course of what others have had to face. All you need to remember is that God will never let you down; he'll never let you be pushed past your limit; he'll always be there to help you come through it.

—*The Message Remix*, 1 Corinthians 10:13

When you stand firm, you will never regret it. He may pout, stomp, threaten, get angry, or even break up with you. No matter how high he turns up the heat, don't cave in under pressure. The more times you choose the right thing, the easier it is to continue to do the right thing. Make the right choice. Be true to yourself. Even though you may lose this guy as a "friend," you're actually doing him a favor. By resisting temptation, you are keeping two people from making a mistake and suffering the consequences.

WHY are EmOtions SO InVOLved in having Sex?

Answer:

Emotions are so involved in having sex because emotions are an important part of intimacy. <u>Sex involves your mind, your body, and your emotions.</u> Sex without emotions would be animalistic.

Let's Talk

Sex involves emotional as well as physical intimacy. It is personal and private. You cannot separate the physical from the emotional closeness, because that's the way God designed it—especially for girls. We deeply desire to bond with another person and live happily ever after. As we expose our heart, body, and mind to another person, we take the risk of being rejected. Don't let your emotions rule your physical actions. Don't fool yourself into thinking that you can just be physical without getting involved emotionally. It's just not true!

As you draw a physical boundary line for what you will and will not do with a guy, draw an emotional boundary line. Determine that you will not give your heart away to a guy before you are ready for marriage. Even though you like him, don't let your emotions take you down the aisle too soon. Keep thinking with your mind, not your feelings.

Life has taught us that love does not consist in gazing at each other, but in looking outward together in the same direction.

—Antoine de Saint-Exupery,
Wind, Sand, and Stars

● ●

Does having SEX the 1st time HURT?

Answer:
It depends. Having sex for the first time may be a bit uncomfortable.

Let's Talk

There are many physical factors that determine whether or not having sex will hurt. These factors are unique to each individual and situation. If you are a virgin when you get married, there is a possibility that your hymen, the membrane covering your vagina, will still be intact. If so, the first time you have sex, it will break and may hurt a little. However, using tampons may cause some girls' hymens to spontaneously break without them realizing it.

It'll Be Right When You're Ready

A lot of women experience pain when they start having sex because their bodies aren't used to it. Some girls' vaginas are smaller or bigger than others, and frankly, some guys' penises are smaller or bigger than others. Depending on the combination of the two of you, it may or may not hurt. Some people experience no discomfort at all right from the start, and for others it takes time to get used to each other's bodies. Even if it hurts at first, it won't hurt forever. Your body will adapt.

Many times, sex hurts because a young woman simply isn't ready. She needs time to become aroused. It is then that her vagina expands and becomes naturally lubricated. A man can be ready for sex as soon as he gets an erection. Sometimes the man gets too excited and tries to enter the woman before her body is ready for him. In this case, it will hurt. This often happens when girls have sex before they are married. Since the man has no real commitment to the woman, he may not take the time to tend to her needs before his own. However, when you are married, your husband is committed to you and should want to make sure you are ready and comfortable.

"Tick-Tock"

Save Sex

Saving sex for marriage means that you are saving one of the most special and intimate acts for someone who really loves and cares about you. This is important because sex makes you very vulnerable. You are totally exposed, and that can be kind of embarrassing, not to mention messy. This means that <u>someone else knows you intimately enough that they could hurt you emotionally.</u> Having vulnerability with your husband actually strengthens your marriage bond. The two of you share something special.

Don't give away your gift!!

47

Marriage should be the kind of relationship that allows you to talk about how you are feeling. If sex hurts, or you are not enjoying it, you will be able to talk about what will make it better and how your husband can help you. God created sex to be enjoyed. So even if sex isn't perfect at first, the two of you, as a married couple, can grow together to eventually experience all that sex was intended to be.

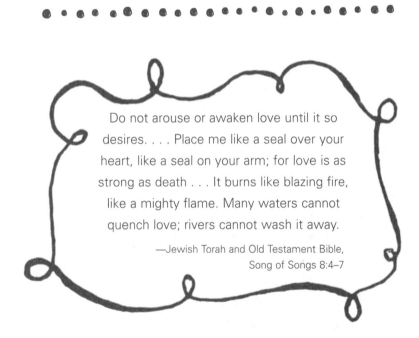

Do not arouse or awaken love until it so desires. . . . Place me like a seal over your heart, like a seal on your arm; for love is as strong as death . . . It burns like blazing fire, like a mighty flame. Many waters cannot quench love; rivers cannot wash it away.

—Jewish Torah and Old Testament Bible,
Song of Songs 8:4–7

WHat are GENITAL WARtS, and How Do you Get tHem?

Answer:

Genital warts are actually caused by human papilloma virus (HPV). This virus also causes 99 percent of all cervical cancer. It's transmitted by skin-to-skin contact with someone else who has it.

Let's Talk

HPV is the fastest growing viral STD in America today. Twenty to forty million Americans have it. By the time girls get to college, 60 percent who are sexually active are infected with HPV. It's nothing to mess around with. No matter how hot that guy looks to you, having sex with him is *not* a risk worth taking. And it's not just sex that transmits this disease— you can get it simply by skin-to-skin contact of the infected areas. So condoms won't even provide full protection.

Once you have HPV, you can never get rid of it. You will deal with it for the rest of your life. It takes your time, energy, and money. Instead of hanging out with your friends, you may be spending your time at the doctor's office, enduring hours of probing, prodding, and medical testing. That's probably not the way you want to spend the rest of your life!

Symptoms for Life

One to six months after being exposed to HPV, a girl (or guy) may experience the first outbreak of genital warts. These ugly bumps will cause burning and itching down there. Warts can also appear in the mouth or on the lips, tongue, and throat (more icky consequences of

oral sex). Sometimes the warts can go away by themselves, but the most common treatment is a prescription cream. The last resort is the horrifying experience of having a doctor freeze them off with liquid nitrogen or having them surgically removed. So keep your private parts private. The physical consequences of living with HPV are painful, inconvenient, and embarrassing.

I loved thee once, I'll love no more,
Thine be the grief as is the blame,
Thou are not what thou wast before—
What reason I should be the same?

—Sir Robert Aytoun,
"To an Inconstant Mistress"

If a Teenage GIRL isn't MaRRieD & gets PRegNant, should she Have an ABORTION, KeEp her BABY, or give her baby up 4 ADOPTION?

Answer:

Every child deserves a chance, so it's better to carry your baby to full term and then give it up for adoption.

Let's Talk

Nobody expects a teenage girl to raise a baby. Keeping a baby while trying to finish high school is an honorable thought, but it's unrealistic unless you have lots of help and

support from your family. Your dreams, goals, and future plans will be squelched because all of your time will be spent taking care of your baby. Babies are cute, but they demand 100 percent of a mom's time and attention.

Nine out of ten guys abandon their pregnant girlfriends.

Adoption Is the Answer

Carrying an unwanted pregnancy to full term and lovingly giving the baby to a couple to raise and nurture is a great way to handle a teen pregnancy. Having a baby before you are married can be embarrassing and inconvenient. You might lose your friends, your freedom, and your future. Your parents will probably be disappointed in you. Placing your child up for adoption is the best solution.

Many couples experience the frustration of infertility and are unable to have children. In some places, the waiting list for adopting a baby is very long. The process may take years. Some couples go outside of the United States to find a baby because of the shortage. These people really, really, really want a baby. The greatest gift you could ever give someone is the gift of life. What a blessing your unplanned pregnancy could be for a couple that has the resources and desire to provide and care for your baby. Although nine months of pregnancy may seem like an eternity of discomfort and embarrassment, it's nothing compared to a lifetime of regret.

Don't Abort Your Baby

Even though abortion seems like a quick fix, it can have lasting physical, emotional, and spiritual consequences on the mother. Teens that have abortions sometimes find it difficult to conceive children later in life. The process itself can cause internal scarring and seriously damage the reproductive system. Many girls also report emotional consequences of shame, guilt, grief, sadness, and thoughts of suicide.

Life begins at conception; the baby is equipped with everything he or she needs to become a full-grown person. Research shows that a baby's heart begins beating between fourteen and twenty-one days, before you even realize you are pregnant. Unborn babies deserve to live, to experience all that God has intended for them. Having an abortion destroys two lives—the baby's and the mother's.

FACT

Since 1973, over thirty million abortions have occurred in America. One-fourth are performed on teen girls.

Norma McCorvey (Jane Roe), the woman whose case got abortion legalized in the U.S. in 1973, is now strongly against abortion. She works toward reversing the legalization of abortion by telling her story of regret all over the country. She speaks to women and teenagers about the emotional consequences abortion brings.

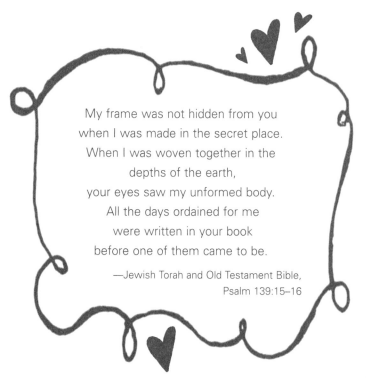

My frame was not hidden from you
when I was made in the secret place.
When I was woven together in the
depths of the earth,
your eyes saw my unformed body.
All the days ordained for me
were written in your book
before one of them came to be.

—Jewish Torah and Old Testament Bible,
Psalm 139:15–16

Can You get PReGNaNT EvEn if YOU use A condom?

Answer:
Yes.

Let's Talk

There's a one in twenty chance that a condom will not work—it may break or tear, and you might get pregnant. If you're married and use a condom as birth control, you'll be surprised if you get pregnant, but you'll be in a better position to handle it. If you're not married, it's a different story. Let's get real. Are you in a position to raise a family?

FACT

Condoms have between a 10 and 20 percent failure rate in preventing pregancy. This means that out of a hundred kids in your class, twenty of you could be condom babies. Wow!

Condoms Are Not Guaranteed

Worrying about a condom leaking when you have sex does not make the act very enjoyable.

Not every condom is tested for holes. In fact, one out of five condom batches fails to meet U.S. standards. Plus, condoms that are carried around in pockets or wallets often get damaged. A broken condom could be the first step down the road of emotional breakdown. There is no condom in the world that can protect your heart. Abstinence before marriage is the only way to guarantee you won't get pregnant.

> **FACT**
>
> On a positive note, when used correctly, condoms can help prevent pregnancy and STDs. They just aren't completely foolproof!

You have kissed and nibbled and poked and prodded and worried me there so often that my virginity was lost in the shuffle.

—Vladimir Nabokov,
Ada, or Ardor: A Family Chronicle

WHAT is HERPES, & how DO YOU get it?

Answer:

Herpes is an extremely contagious virus that causes outbreaks of painful blisters. It is passed from one person to another by skin-to-skin contact with the infected area. Most people who develop herpes will continue to have outbreaks for the rest of their lives.

Let's Talk

Studies show that herpes victims have overwhelming feelings of guilt, anger, and helplessness. Girls with herpes blame themselves and feel powerless. They have a disease that can't be cured by a pill or a shot, and there's nothing they can do to stop it. They live with the guilt of knowing they could pass the virus on to someone else. Even an unborn baby can contract herpes from its mother, resulting in permanent brain damage, blindness, or death.

You Own It for Life

Herpes can be treated, *but there is no cure*. Flu-like symptoms develop and small painful blisters appear on your privates two to twenty days after you are infected. Blisters cause pain for several weeks and then disappear, laying low until the next episode. Outbreaks can be triggered by stress, fatigue, illness, or even sunburn. Most people with genital herpes have about five to eight outbreaks a year. Herpes can spread from person to person during skin-to-skin contact of the infected area, even when the sores or symptoms aren't there. Some types of medications can reduce the outbreaks, but once you've got herpes, you own it for life!

What attracts us in a woman
rarely binds us to her.

—John Churton Collins, Literary Critic

WHEN YOU HAVE **SEX** 4 the **1**ST TiMe, HOW DO YOU KNOW WHAT 2 DO, and HOW DO YOU BECOME EXPERIENCED ?

Answer:

You won't know what to do the first time you have sex. However, you can choose to become experienced inside the safety of marriage, with one man who is committed to you, or you can choose to become experienced outside of marriage, with a guy you may never even see again. You will be able to trust your husband, but there is no guarantee your boyfriend will be around tomorrow.

Let's Talk

You've probably seen sex scenes on TV or in movies, but those are all scripted and choreographed. They may look natural and spontaneous, but they probably shot the scene a hundred times to get it right! You will never really know what it's like until you experience it. Sex is awkward, and most people are unsure, embarrassed, and self-conscious at first.

Sex is designed to be a journey married couples enjoy together, learning as they go. Sex is something to look forward to. You don't have to be an expert on your honeymoon. Part of the excitement of beginning life as a couple is learning about sex together and guiding and helping each other along the way. When you're married, you have the security to be yourself, admit what you don't know, and enjoy discovering each other together. Sex may not be everything you imagined at first, but it's designed to get better as you go.

"Emotional Baggage Inside"

The Myth

It's a myth that being sexually experienced before marriage improves your relationship. It does not. It actually creates a lot of emotional baggage. Many women say they have flashbacks of the first guy they had sex with—and sometimes that was not a good experience! Even after being married for a long time, they can't seem to get that first time out of their mind.

Save your first sexual experience for the one you
walk down the aisle with.

Who will in time present
from pleasure refrain,
shall in time to come,
the more pleasure obtain.

—John Heywood,
*A Dialogue Containing the Number in Effect
of the Effectual, Proverbs in the English Tongue*

What Should You do If A RElAtivE or other ADULT is Touching YOU in a SEXUAL way and TelLs you 2 Keep IT secret?

Answer:

Tell your parents, youth leader, school counselor, or someone else you trust as soon as possible. Get help and refuse to allow it to continue.

Let's Talk

If someone violates you, you are not the one at fault. This person should be arrested. Do not be embarrassed or ashamed, and above all, <u>do not allow it to continue</u>. Tell your parents or someone you trust so you can be safe and get out of the situation.

Protect Yourself

Stay away from this person! Do not allow this person to come into your room or your house. Refuse to go to this person's house, and refuse to pretend that what he or she is doing is okay. You must protect yourself from further harm. If you need help, notify the police and get their assistance. Kick, bite, yell, scream, and refuse to be a victim!

Get Help

Girls that hide abuse suffer emotional pain later on in life. They may even have difficulty enjoying sex with their husbands after they are married because they feel dirty or shameful. It's best to talk about it, process it, and receive healing. You've been wronged. Get counseling immediately. Instead of being a victim, choose to become victorious.

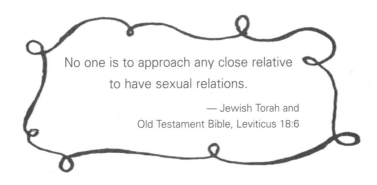

No one is to approach any close relative to have sexual relations.

— Jewish Torah and
Old Testament Bible, Leviticus 18:6

WHaT aRE DATE RaPe DrUGS ?

Answer:

These drugs are sometimes used to aid a person in taking sexual advantage of a girl. This is called sexual assault.

Let's Talk

Sexual assault is any type of sexual activity that you do not agree to. Date rape drugs tend to make you physically helpless and unable to refuse sex. You usually can't even remember what happened. The drugs often have no color, smell, or taste, and are easily added to flavored drinks without the victim's knowledge. There are at least three main date rape drugs:

- **GHB** (gamma hydroxybutyric acid): GHB has a few forms: a liquid with no odor or color, a white powder, or a pill.

- **Ketamine** (ketamine hydrochloride): Ketamine is a white powder.

● **Rohypnol** (flunitrazepam):
Rohypnol is a pill and dissolves in
liquids. New pills turn blue when
added to liquids. However, the old
pills, with no color, are still available.

How Do They Work?

Date rape drugs can affect you really
quickly. The length of time they last depends
on how much of the drug is taken and if it is
mixed with other things like alcohol. Alcohol
can worsen the drugs' effects and can cause
more health problems. Also, the drug GHB can
be made by people in their homes, so you don't
always know what other things are in it.

Symptoms of Date Rape Drugs

● **GHB:**
drowsiness, unconsciousness, trouble
seeing, nausea, seizures, problems
breathing, tremors, sweating, slow heart
rate, coma, a dreamlike sensation, and
even death

● **Ketamine:**
hallucinations, lost sense of time, distorted
sights and sounds, convulsions, trouble

breathing, vomiting, an out-of-body experience, numbness, aggressive or violent behavior, and slurred speech

● **Rohypnol:**
low blood pressure, muscle relaxation, problems talking, a drunk feeling, confusion, dizziness, problems seeing, not remembering what happened while drugged, and stomach problems

Be SMART

You can protect yourself from becoming a victim of date rape drugs. Don't accept drinks from other people or share drinks. Keep your drink with you at all times, even when you go to the bathroom. Open soda containers yourself and never drink from an open punch bowl at a party. If something smells or tastes strange, don't drink it. (GHB, for instance, sometimes tastes salty.) Always bring a friend with you at a party or get-together, so you can watch out for each other.

Emergency

If you think you may have been drugged and raped, go to the police station or hospital right away. Don't pee until you get help. They will do a urine test to detect the drugs. Most drugs will stay in your body two to seventy-two hours. If you think you've been raped, do not bathe, douche, or change your clothes. These things can give evidence of the rape and help the police catch the criminal.

It is important to get counseling from a trusted professional right away. Feelings of shame, guilt, fear, and shock are normal. Date rape drugs are serious, and they are used to take advantage of girls. Stay alert, be cautious, and most of all, *be smart*!

For the slang & street names for drugs

http://www.pride.org/slangdrugterms.HTM#R

or

http://en.wikipedia.org/wiki/Drug_street_names

National Domestic Violence Hotline
800-799-SAFE or 800-787-3224 (TDD).

My friend was DATe RAPED and Got PREGNANT. Since it WASN'T her FauLt, Is IT OK 4 her to Have an ABORTioN?

Answer:
No, it's not OK to end the baby's life because it was conceived through rape.

Let's Talk
Date rape is a huge violation of a girl's trust and privacy. Any guy who would take advantage of a girl sexually is committing a serious

crime. Dealing with rape is tough enough, but having to deal with a pregnancy because of the violation complicates things even further. Living through nine months of pregnancy and dealing with the daily embarrassment *would* seem to prolong the healing process and make it harder to forgive and forget. However, having an abortion has consequences, too—ones that will

> **FACT.**
>
> Having an abortion can cause major stress called Post-Abortion Syndrome. Some girls that have an abortion experience depression, thoughts of suicide, isolation from their friends, and poor self-esteem.

last far longer than nine months. Think about this: that innocent baby did nothing to deserve the death penalty. That little person might grow up to be the doctor who finds the cure to cancer or AIDS. God has a plan for every soul!

It's a Crime

Encourage your friend to report the crime and get medical attention immediately. Rape can damage the reproductive organs, and although you can get pregnant as soon as you start having your period (eleven to fifteen years of age, for most girls), your body is still not fully developed until your late teens. A violent rape can seriously hurt a girl's developing insides. Next, advise her to seek out an adoption service that can provide prenatal care. Once the baby is born, it can be placed in a loving home.

Get Help!

Any girl who has been raped needs to get professional counseling. She needs to talk with someone who is knowledgeable and trustworthy. The devastating emotional impact of rape can cripple a life forever if it's not dealt with in a healthy way. Encourage your friend not to be ashamed or afraid to tell someone. Keeping it a secret is just as damaging as living with the reality that she's been raped.

A Second Chance

God has a special purpose and plan for every one of us, including your friend and her baby. They both deserve another chance. The baby can be placed in a loving home, and your friend can get help. Technically, if your friend was a virgin, her virginity has been stolen from her. But she doesn't have to feel ashamed—she can reclaim it! Even though the date rape wasn't part of her plans, there can still be hope, healing, and a positive future for everyone involved.

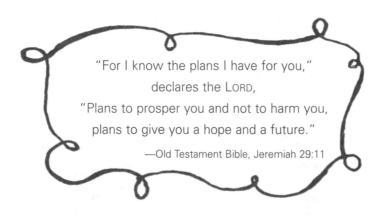

"For I know the plans I have for you,"
declares the LORD,
"Plans to prosper you and not to harm you,
plans to give you a hope and a future."

—Old Testament Bible, Jeremiah 29:11

Does AₗCₒhₒL makE *Sₑχ* beTTER?
Answer:
No.

Let's Talk

Alcohol is a depressant. Depressants do not increase sexual pleasure. Alcohol decreases your inhibitions and your ability to think clearly and make wise decisions. When you drink, you do things you would not normally do. In fact, many incidences of premarital sex and date rape occur when people are under the influence of alcohol.

CAUTION

Don't believe anyone who tells you that they "love you" while drunk.

Be sober-minded and don't drink alcohol until you are twenty-one. Not only is underage drinking illegal, it's really dumb, when you consider the consequences. Don't put yourself in a place or situation where everyone is drinking alcohol, because you could end up giving into the pressure to drink. Be extremely cautious. Know what you're drinking. Don't accept any beverage from another person unless you have watched them pour the drink. Sometimes a guy puts alcohol in a girl's drink without her knowing

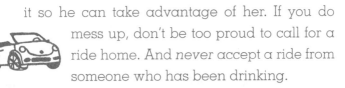

FACT

About one in five teen drivers killed in car crashes were drunk.

it so he can take advantage of her. If you do mess up, don't be too proud to call for a ride home. And *never* accept a ride from someone who has been drinking.

"One reason I don't drink is that I want to know when I am having a good time."

—Nancy Astor, British Politician

Can you get STDs FROM your Husband?

Answer:

Yes and no. Yes, if he has an STD. Even though you are married, you are not prevented from getting disease. No, if you and your husband are both virgins and you both remain completely faithful to each other after you are married.

Let's Talk

The act of getting married does not take away the consequences of having made a bad choice in the past. That's why it's so important to realize how your choices today affect the rest of your life. When you do get into a serious relationship and start talking marriage, you and your boyfriend will need to have some very open conversations about any past sexual relationships.

It might not seem very romantic, but a visit to the doctor for a full check-up before the wedding is probably a good idea if you have a history.

Wouldn't it be awesome to marry someone who had remained sexually pure just like you? Truthfully, this is the only real way to ensure you will not get an STD. When you both choose to remain sexually pure before and during marriage, you avoid a lot of heartache and enjoy a relationship based on trust. You know that when you make love with him, you have nothing to worry about. Neither one of you are thinking about other people you've had sex with, and you're not wondering how you measure up.

"Wisdom consists of the anticipation of consequences."

—Norman Cousins, *Saturday Review*

Can you get PREgNANT if YOU have SEX during your PeriOd?

Answer:
Yes.

Let's Talk

Each woman has a slightly different monthly cycle, but generally one egg is released from a woman's ovaries about every twenty-eight days. If you start counting day one as the first day of your period, the next egg is released from your ovaries fourteen to sixteen days later. This is the most likely window of time you can become pregnant, if you have a regular twenty-eight-day cycle. Realistically, each woman is different. If you have a thirty-day cycle, your fertile day might be day eighteen. Unfortunately, you never know the length of your cycle until your period finally hits again. The egg lives for twenty-four hours before it starts to break up and cannot be fertilized. However, a sperm can live three to five days. Even if you have sex before day fourteen of your cycle, those sperm will happily live in your vaginal mucus for several days waiting for the next egg to get released. And remember, it only takes one sperm out of millions ejaculated to start a pregnancy.

- Girls are born with about 450,000 eggs.

- There are 200–600 million sperm in one ejaculation! Wow!

- Men's supply of sperm is continually replenished; production continues throughout their whole adult life.

During your period, your body is flushing out the uterus lining and shedding the unfertilized egg that was released that month. However, some girls have irregular periods, bleeding, or spotting. You may mistake this as your period. It *is* possible to get pregnant during this time if an egg has been released. Countless girls have gotten pregnant during the first month of their very first period—and in some cases—the very first time they had sex. Yikes!

HoW do yOu KNOW when You've FouND **MR.** Right ?

Answer:

You know he's the right guy for you when he meets all of your criteria, and you are in a position where you can make a permanent marriage commitment (old enough to have a job, buy a house, and take care of a baby).

Let's Talk

Nobody's perfect, but there are several guys in this world who would be a good match for you. It's not too early to begin creating a list of must–haves and can't–stands in a life partner.

Chemistry is always the first thing that we use to judge attraction. It's natural. There are lots of hot guys out there, but they are not all husband material. You do need chemistry, but if that's all you've got, the relationship will definitely end in divorce. Be careful to look beyond the physical traits and stay true to your list of criteria. Studies show that the more similar you are, the better the match is. In other words, opposites do *not* attract! The best partnerships are when both people come from the same kind of family background, from the same religion,

FACT

- Couples who report being the happiest are the ones who like doing the same kinds of recreational activities together!
- Getting married as a teenager is the highest known risk factor of divorce!
- People who wait and get married until after they are twenty-five years old have happier marriages and are less likely to divorce.
- People who have college educations report more satisfying marriages and are less likely to divorce.
- Sixty percent of married people were introduced to each other by a friend or family member.

and from a similar economic status. Your perfect guy should have a similar energy level and personality type, and love doing the same things you enjoy.

Next, ask yourself what your parents would think of him. Your parents usually want what's best for you, and don't want to see you settle for anything less. If they don't like him, life could get difficult. He will probably spend a lot of time with your family after you get married. Your parents' approval or disapproval can greatly affect the happiness of your marriage.

Take a look at his character. Is he honest, faithful, trustworthy, kind, gentle, and patient? Does he have self-control? If the answer is yes, he might be a keeper. If not, throw him back . . . there are a lot more fish in the sea. Don't feel the need to rush. The longer you get to know him, the more you'll learn about his real character traits, strengths, and weaknesses.

That's a No-Brainer

WARNING

Never get involved with someone who has an addiction, is a druggie or an alcoholic, has a mental disorder, or is involved in criminal activity.

First, Know Who You Are

Two complete people will have a better chance for a successful marriage than two people who are still trying to find themselves. Always strive to learn more about who you are, and what your own likes, dislikes, and goals are. If you have a firm idea of where you are going, you will be more likely to choose someone who is similar and wants the same types of things.

It is confidence in our
bodies, minds, and spirits
that allows us to keep looking for
new adventures, new directions to grow in,
and new lessons to learn—
which is what life is all about.

–Oprah Winfrey, Talk Show Host

SOURCES

Cohen, Abraham. *Everyman's Talmud: The Major Teachings of the Rabbinic Sages.* New York: Schocken Books Inc., 1949.

Cox, Melissa P., ed. *Questions Kids Ask About Sex: Honest Answers for Every Age.* Austin, Texas: Medical Institute for Sexual Health, 2005.

Di Marco, Hayley. *The Dirt on Dating: A Dateable Book.* Grand Rapids, Mich.: Revell, 2004.

Feminist Women's Health Center. *Menstrual Cycles: What Really Happens in Those 28 Days?!* Tacoma, Washington. http://www.fwhc.org

Gray, John. *Men Are From Mars, Women Are From Venus: A Practical Guide for Improving Communication and Getting What You Want in Your Relationships.* New York: Harper Collins, 1992.

Kirgiss, Crystal and Pam Stenzil. *Sex Has a Price Tag: Discussions About Sexuality, Spirituality, and Self Respect.* Grand Rapids, Michigan: Zondervan, 2002.

SOURCES

Kirgiss, Crystal. *What's Up With Boys: Everything You Need to Know About Guys*. Grand Rapids, Michigan: Zondervan, 2004.

Linfield, Jordan and Joseph Krivisky. *Words of Love*. New York: Random House, 2001.

Lookadoo, Justin. *The Dirt on Sex: A Datable Book*. Grand Rapids, Mich.: Revell, 2004.

Meeker, Meg, M.D. *Epidemic: Raising Great Teens in a Toxic Sexual Culture*. Washington, D.C.: Lifeline Press, 2002.

Yusuf Ali, Abdullah, trans. and Sayed A.A. Razwy, ed., *The Qur'an Translation*. Elmhurst, N.Y.: Tahrike Tarsile Qur'an, Inc., 1990.

The Torah (trans.). Great Britain: Labyrinth Publishing Ltd., 1996.

U.S. Department of Health and Human Services. Center for Disease Control. "Sexually Transmitted Diseases." http://www.cdc.gov

U.S. Department of Health and Human Services. Office on Women's Health. "Date Rape Drugs." Washington, D.C. http://www.womenshealth.gov

Gina Guddat, the primary writer behind *Unwrapped*, is the founder and executive director of F.I.T. Decisions Foundation and the Girls Only Conferences. As a writer, speaker, fitness instructor, and personal trainer, Gina has been involved in teaching women and teen girls about health and wellness since 1985. She has three beautiful daughters, ages thirteen, fifteen, and seventeen. Her desire is for her own girls to know the truth, the whole truth, and nothing but the truth about God's awesome gift of sex. She sees *Unwrapped* as a tangible way to make certain young women everywhere are informed and equipped with the knowledge they will need for a successful future.

Nancy Fehrmann is a wife, mother, grandmother, and registered nurse with a passion for empowering women with truth. *Unwrapped* is her original inspiration, and the source of its medical accuracy. The many hours she has poured into this project are a true display of her love for teen girls. Nancy teaches, motivates, encourages, and equips girls and young women across the country, helping them to make wise and healthy decisions regarding dating, boys, boundaries, and purity.

Lydia Cole is a wife, mother, registered nurse, and educator. She is also a marathon runner, tennis instructor, and triathlete. In 1998, she won the Mrs. Alabama/America Pageant. Lydia's love and concern for teens shows in her contributions to *Unwrapped*. She works as a mentor to young girls in the areas of self-image, purity, and goal-setting, providing them with information and practical tools.

Angela Ramsey is a writer, education specialist, and organizational consultant for F.I.T. Decisions. Angela has worked directly with young people as an educator in both the public school and church arenas. In the role of consultant, Angela has assisted F.I.T. Decisions in writing and editing their manuscripts, including *Unwrapped*. Over the past two decades, Angela has authored and co-authored numerous educational curriculums and Bible studies. She is currently working on a series of novels for middle school and high school teenagers.

Lainey Guddat, a high school senior, helped to edit and review the book *Unwrapped*. She's involved in honors classes and proudly brags about her completion of advanced placement calculus (the hardest academic experience of her life). In her free time, she enjoys reading, writing, running, and singing in the choir. She has grandiose plans for the future—graduation, college, leading the industrialized world—but for now, she's just floating along and taking things in. After all, the only way a person can learn is by paying attention to what is going on around them. She urges readers to listen to and learn from this book, and she feels privileged to have taken part in its creation.

Angela Mathena is a wife, mother, and professional artist. She teaches art, serves in her church, and coaches her daughter's soccer team. A small business owner, Angela has utilized her graphic design training and talent to inspire the artistic content of *Unwrapped*. The cover concept, photos, and doodles were her inspiration. She is excited about this creative way of giving young women the information they need to succeed in life. Angela's philosophy is: "All you have to decide is what to do with the time that is given to you" (J. R. R. Tolkien).

About F.I.T. Decisions Foundation

The mission of F.I.T. Decisions is to educate and motivate teens to pursue total spiritual, social, emotional, and physical fitness. "F.I.T." stands for the Future Identity of Teens. The organization strongly believes that the decisions teenagers make today can positively affect the rest of their lives. F.I.T. Decisions' Girls Only Conferences are designed to provide girls with opportunities to understand and evaluate the benefits and consequences of their decisions, and learn to make healthy choices for a successful future.

**For more questions or to schedule a
Girls Only Conference in your city,
call 1-888-232-0222, contact us at
Gina@fitdecisions.org,
or visit our Web sites:
www.fitdecisions.org
www.girlsonlyconference.org**

Everything you are and do from fifteen
to eighteen is what you are and will
do the rest of your life.

—F. Scott Fitzgerald, Writer
(in a letter to his daughter, dated September 19,1938)